Home Reflections: Or Ashford, Past And Present

Robert Furley

The following proposal for establishing a Hospital

HOME REFLECTIONS;

OR

ASHFORD,

PAST AND PRESENT,

BY

ROBERT FURLEY.

AN ADDRESS

DELIVERED AT THE PUBLIC ROOMS, ASHFORD,

ON WEDNESDAY, THE 16TH OCTOBER, 1867,

In aid of the Funds of the South Ashford District Visiting Society.

ASHFORD:

Printed and Published by H. IGGLESDEN, at the KENTISH EXPRESS and ASHFORD NEWS Office, and may be had of all Booksellers.

1867.

HOME REFLECTIONS.

The autumn is drawing to a close, winter is returning, with it our long evenings, and those who are disposed to throw into a common stock, and for the benefit of others, any powers of amusement or improvement which they may possess, should not be charged with vanity, but hailed as the promoters of mutual fellowship. With this feeling I present myself before you this evening. My subject shall be " Home Reflections—Ashford, as it was, and as it is." It is generally supposed that Wye was formerly a more important place than Ashford, and that the town of Wye once stood near Pett Street, between Wye and Crundale; it has also been surmised that the Romans had a highway through it, in the direction of Lenham. The main road from Maidstone to the coast subsequently brought Ashford more into the world, and Wye went back. At the latter end of the summer of 1625 the plague raged dreadfully in Ashford and its vicinity, and the inhabitants being unable to support the sick, the neighbouring district was by an Order of the Privy Council, taxed for that purpose, " lest the sick should be forced for the succour of their lives to break forth of the town, to the great danger of the country." Ashford, like Wye, had its College; but no remarkable men, or events, appear to have brought either place into much note, except Cardinal Kemp, the founder of Wye College, who was born at Wye in 1380 and died a Cardinal of the Church of Rome as well as Archbishop of Canterbury, and from whom Kemp's Corner derives its name. Ashford once possessed a Knight in the person of Sir John Fogge, who died in 1490, and was a liberal benefactor to the Church. Sir Norton Knatchbull erected the School House in the reign of Charles the 1st. We have a few benefactions in trust for the poor of the parish, including four almshouses in Tufton-street, erected in 1853 partly from the legacy given by the late Mr. James Wall and partly by public subscription. An endowment of these almshouses has been since commenced by Mr. Thomas Whitfeld of Lewes, with a gift of £100. We have also a lying-in charity, at present under the management of Mrs. Alcock and a committee ; and a clothing club, under the management of the Misses Whitfeld and a committee. About thirty-five years ago a benevolent society was formed to sell bread and coal to the poor during inclement seasons at reduced prices ; Mr. Thorpe, sen., is the treasurer. These with the District Visiting Societies, of which more hereafter, constitute the charities of the town. Ashford some seventy years ago had the character of being "a small but neat and cheerful Town, and many of the inhabitants of a genteel rank in life." During the wars of the First Napoleon, barracks were constructed at Ashford and Brabourne. The barracks were built in the year 1805, at Barrow Hill, and taken down at the close of the war. The morality of the place, as a matter of course, was not thereby improved. The large residence of the late Mr. Mascall now forms the site of four dwelling houses. Other old family residences have also been converted into places of business,—nearly every one now residing here, is engaged in some worldly pursuit ; and what is remarkable, with two or three exceptions, there is not a house in the town occupied by the same proprietor who held it forty years ago.

In extent the parish is not large, there being only 2,786 acres in it. By the kindness of the Registrar-General I am enabled to supply you with the population census during the present century:

1801	......	2,151	1841	......	3,082
1811	......	2,532	1851	......	5,007
1821	......	2,773	1861	......	6,950
1831	......	2,809			

Thus it will be seen that the population in 1861 was more than three times as large as in 1801, and that there was *no* material change between 1811 and 1841, and that it was more than doubled between 1841 and 1861, and now it is supposed to exceed 8,000.

Our mornings are still ushered in by the five o'clock bell, and while the shades of evening close around us, the Conqueror's badge of servitude, "the solemn curfew," may still be heard. The morning bell is no doubt useful to the mechanic, but thirty years ago it was equally useful to the enterprising individual who contemplated a journey to London and back the same day; for he had, at the sound of this bell to shake off *his drowsiness*, and prepare for a journey in Mr. Francis Packham's Van to Maidstone. This started about six, and the proprietor did all in his power to amuse his passengers during their tedious journey. At Maidstone you were taken on by coach to London, and arrived there (if the roads were good) by about one o'clock and had two hours to transact business in London: at three you returned the same way, and reached Ashford about ten at night, thus devoting fourteen hours in travelling, to gain two hours in London. What would be said of this, in these go-ahead days? About ten o'clock the old Folkestone coach made its appearance at the Saracen's Head on its way to London, and many were the heads thrust out of doors and windows to behold *one of the great events of the day.* There were two coaches on the road, one leaving London, and the other Folkestone, daily; the coach from London reached Ashford about four, and as the fiery chestnuts came round the Castle corner, many an idler rushed to the Saracen's Head for the latest intelligence from the great city, and to get a sight of one solitary copy of *The Times* for the use of the whole town. The drivers of these coaches, (poor Richardson and Wallace), were great favorites with the public, but like most favorites, they were spoilt, and when their daily occupation was gone they were soon forgotten. Each mid-day witnessed the arrival of the different vans from the cross-roads, and as they occupied the space under the Public Rooms, some little bustle was occasioned thereby. Would the public like to return to this state of things?

The Cattle Market (of which more anon), then held in the town on the first and third Tuesday, was the most important event of the week.

SELECT VESTRY, SIR FRANCIS HEAD AND THE "QUARTERLY REVIEW," POOR LAW SYSTEM.

Next in importance were the weekly proceedings of the select vestry—*and* the Ashford of olden time might well be proud of its select vestry, for 'ere it closed its triumphant career, its fame was recorded in one of the leading periodicals of the day, the *Quarterly Review*. The due and proper administration of the Poor Laws is a subject dear to every Englishman. The dissolution of the monasteries in the reign of Henry VIII. threw the maintenance of the poor on the public at large, and in this as in many other worldly matters, *if* the mutual obligations between man and man were faithfully observed, no law would be required to *enforce them*. In the reign of Elizabeth, the first tax was laid upon property for the support of the poor, and it should be ever kept in view that though a parochial assessment endeavours to make a just and equal charge on all property for the maintenance of the poor (on the assumption that there shall be no such thing as actual destitution) still, it in no way relieves any one from the obligation of that private charity which the Christian dispensation has so beautifully developed. But I must hasten on. From the close of the war in 1815 to the year 1818 a number of unemployed, idle, and dissolute men sought parochial relief, and Ashford soon felt the effect of it. Many of the neighbouring landed proprietors also pulled down the cottages on their estates without rebuilding them, and thus drove the less deserving of their poor into this and neighbouring towns, often to live in idleness. The result was that in the year 1818 Ashford, with a population of 2,500, expended no less than £3,450 on its poor, of which £1,212 was applied in weekly relief. This state of things aroused the ratepayers, and a select vestry was formed who met weekly, and by their steady and unwearied exertions they had, when the New Poor Law came into operation, reduced both these items to less than one-third—the amount expended in that year (1834-5) being only £1160, and the weekly relief only £358. Had the same course been pursued in other parishes, the Poor Law Act would have been uncalled for. Idleness, deceit, and peculation were demoralizing the people. The introduction of machinery in agriculture had caused a rising amongst the poor in 1830—the machines were destroyed, incendiary fires followed, and notwithstanding the powerful opposition of *The Times*, the wise provisions of the Act of 1834 became the law of the land. Under that Act Sir Francis Head was appointed one of the assistant Poor Law Commissioners, and this county was assigned to him to form into unions. For the information of the young, I will state that our old parish workhouse stood at the end of New-rents, adjoining the fire-engine house, where, weekly, from the year 1818 to 1835, the members of the select vestry regularly attended. Sir Francis Head was present at one of these meetings, and took notes of what passed, which he afterwards published in the *Quarterly Review* in a paper on "English Charity." His report is a most interesting document, especially to those connected with this town. The late Mr. Richard Greenhill was the chairman on that occasion (and a better one could not have been found as he was foremost to uphold the character of his native town), Mr. Richard Thorpe and Mr. William Morley were the overseers, and out of the sixteen members then present that evening only Mr. Bayley, Mr. Richard Lewis (then the churchwarden), Messrs. Benjamin and Richard Thorpe, and Mr. Thomas Thurston, are now residing in the town : the destroying hand of time has removed seven, viz., Messrs. Richard Greenhill, William Walter, William Parnell, Walter Murton, John Hutton, John Worger, and George Halbertson, and the four who have left the town are Messrs. Stephen Tunbridge, William

Scott, George James Morgan, and William Morley. In this publication Sir Francis Head says: "The system of administering relief to the poor in the parish and town of Ashford is so creditable to East Kent, it has produced such beneficial effects, and it offers such valuable instruction to the Poor Law Commissioners, as well as to the country in general, that it may be useful to lay before the public a short account of it." It would be tedious to detail here the proceedings and mode of dealing with the applicants for relief *as* reported by Sir Francis. The most scrutinizing inquiries he states were made, and in several cases attempts at imposition were detected, exposed, and the claim refused. In short he goes on to say: "Every applicant had the advantage of appearing before a well educated jury of practical men, who, as far as he was capable of judging, seemed determined to administer justice with mercy. The moral effect of this sensible, humane, and business like system, it is almost impossible for any one, however deeply he may have considered the subject, to calculate. Many who would not hesitate to be beggars in private would shrink from the disgrace of being mendicants in public. On the other hand, the widow, the orphan, the person really in want, had in their favour a tribunal in which the best ingredients of the English character were undoubtedly to be found." He closes his remarks by stating, "It is almost needless to add that if every parish had bestowed the same attention on their poor as the parish of Ashford, the Poor Law Amendment Act might instantly be repealed, and its Commissioners, their secretary, and their assistants, scattered like chaff before the wind; but I regret to say that the parish of Ashford is but an 'Oasis in the Desert.'" Now, this honorable distinction was published to the world by an intelligent public officer who had never been in the place before. All honor then to the names of the surviving members of the old select vestry, and to the memory of those who are no more; for it was not the result of a year or two's labour and perseverance which effected this great reduction in the local burthens of the place, but the steady, united, untiring exertions for a period of nearly twenty years of men who had each their own daily callings; and it ought to stimulate the rising generation to follow in the steps of their forefathers, regardless of the taunts and sneers of those who, ever ready to find fault with others, will do nothing themselves for the public good. As an honorable distinction to the town, Sir Francis Head, in forming the East and West Ashford Unions, omitted it from both, and recommended the Commissioners not to disturb the select vestry. However, the inhabitants did not long covet this honorable distinction, and soon petitioned to be united to the West Ashford Union. The first guardians were the late Mr. William Walter and Mr. Mark Dorman, who were members of the old vestry and had for many years devoted their time to the business of the town. Mr. Thorpe, sen. and Mr. Lepine subsequently filled the office; and when Mr. Thorpe retired in 1863 a dinner was given to him, and a cup and salver presented to him for having served the town in various ways for forty years. Ashford is now represented by three guardians (Messrs. Dorman, Norwood, and Greenhill); Mr. A. Briggs was the clerk for about twenty-five years, and that office is now held by Mr. Edward Norwood, of Charing. The rateable value of the property in the parish now amounts to £25,560. The Union expenditure at Lady Day last, amounted for the year to about £2,600, of which £480 was for the contribution from this town to the county rate, £53 for the cattle plague rate, and £2,088 for out-relief, in-maintenance, and Union charges. Of the present system (which like everything else requires judicious periodical revision) I will here only express my regret that the evil resulting from permitting the young to associate with the old and abandoned inmates of both sexes, and thus become early acquainted with vice, still exists. With every precaution, how can it be otherwise? And I should rejoice to see the day when a separate establishment for the Union children of the whole or a portion of the county was formed, with a certain number of acres of land attached to it, and where the children could be better educated at the same, if not less, expense; where the numbers would create emulation; the master and mistresses selected from a superior class; where trades could be taught, and the clothing made for the children and inmates of other Unions. These young people could then procure better situations and be better fitted to contend with the world and its temptations than they are at present. The poor of Ashford have always been well cared for, and perhaps no family looked more after them for thirty years in the present century than the Misses Stoddart and their late brothers. But I must hasten on.

LOCAL ACT OF 1824.

In the year 1824 the first step was taken towards placing the management of the town in the hands of the inhabitants, and an Act was then passed for lighting and watching it. The first Commissioners were appointed by the Act, and as they died off the survivors elected their successors, the ratepayers having no voice in the matter. This was very properly considered a grievance. Under this Act, oil lamps (few and far between) were erected, and in the first instance night, and subsequently day, watchmen were appointed. In the year 1832 the oil lamp was extinguished by the modern and more brilliant gas light, and in the year 1857 that correct personation of the Beadle-Bumble, poor old Gilham, and his comrades, were swept away and the Kent County Constabulary were introduced.

LOCAL BOARD.

The roads of the parish are not of great extent, and at this period were managed under the provisions of the Highway Acts, except those connected with the five turnpike roads, each terminating at the different entrances to the town. Thus matters stood, until the spring of 1863, when the Justices of the county were proceeding to put the New Highway Act into operation, and they proposed to include Ashford in one of the districts. This was displeasing to the ratepayers, who considered the town had now become of sufficient importance to be entrusted with the sole management of its own affairs, and they memorialized the Government to be allowed to adopt the provisions of the

recent Local Government Act, which was granted to them.
A Board of twenty-one inhabitants (elected by the ratepayers) held their first meeting on the 1st of May, 1863,
and the Old Local Act of 1824 was repealed. Mr. George
Lepine was elected the first Chairman, and still holds that
office. One-third, or seven of the members, retire every
year, but they can be re-elected. The Act has been in
operation more than four years, and the public can now
form some opinion of the working of it. The powers of
the Board are great, and if not exercised with sound judgment, they will prove anything but a boon to the town. It
is by matured, and well digested plans, that the lighting,
drainage, paving, and removal of nuisances, the securing a
good supply of water, and carrying out other improvements,
can be effected, and these should all be done gradually,
and so as not to press heavily on the ratepayers in any one
year; and when done they will not be of much avail if the
several occupiers of property do not co-operate with the
Board in connecting drains from their respective premises
with the main drains, and doing all in their power to pro-
mote cleanliness and health. It should always, however,
be kept in view, that an increase in our local burthens,
without an increase of the means of paying them, soon
brings a town to poverty.

MARKETS.

All the different markets of the town, though originally
chartered as far back as the reign of Henry III, were
deemed but of little note until the latter part of the last
century, when increased importance and value were attached
to the grazing land in Romney Marsh, and the different
approaches to the town by means of hard roads were materially improved. This led to the establishment of the
stock market eighty-three years ago, and it was held on the
first and third Tuesdays in the month, in the High Street.
The great promoter of this movement (as well as of the
improvement of the roads), was the late Mr. Henry Creed.
Corn here as in other towns was formerly sold by bulk and
pitched in the market. A room was now opened at the

Royal Oak Inn and the sale by sample was substituted. The corn market was not much frequented, but the stock market grew into importance and became one of the first in the county. At the close of the war the Assembly Rooms, which were erected in 1806, became comparatively useless and so remained until the year 1833. At this time the business of the corn market was increasing, and it was felt that these rooms could not be devoted to a better purpose than by opening them every Tuesday as a corn market. Like most changes, it affected vested rights, and was opposed, and two corn markets were kept open so long back as 1833, and were carried on the same day and hour. The Public Room was subsequently enlarged. The cattle market continued to increase, and in the course of the year 1855 meetings were held to consider the desirability of removing it out of the town. This alteration was not effected without considerable opposition, especially from the leading tradesmen carrying on business in High Street. A suitable site however was obtained as near to the town as possible, and on the 31st July, 1856, the present cattle market, with a siding to the railway, was opened, and a large party, under the able chairmanship of Mr. Harvey, of Godmersham, assembled at the Public Rooms to celebrate the event. Towards the close of 1860 a proposal was set on foot to erect a New Corn Exchange, near the cattle market, with the object of holding the corn market *in the morning*. This proposal met with strong opposition; as, however, the individual who now addresses you took a prominent part in that controversy, it will suffice to state that the New Corn Exchange *was* erected and opened on the 3rd December, 1861, and if the town required a good public room, subsequent events have shown that a New Corn Exchange with a morning market was *not* required. We would, however, hope that all the irritating feelings connected with that undertaking have, after the lapse of nearly seven years, been forgotten, and the public have the advantage of two markets for the sale of corn, one held in the morning and the other in the afternoon. We will return to the more agreeable task of reviewing the success which has attended the New Cattle Market. The Ashford and other Kentish markets were regulated by the calendar month, while the Rye and other Sussex markets were regulated by the lunar month. The long discussion and correspondence respecting the alteration of the days for holding the markets in Kent and Sussex are fresh in the recollection of my hearers, and it only remains for me to say that after frequent attempts to conciliate the supporters of the Rye market, and the threat of opening a fresh market at Ham Street, the Shareholders of the Ashford market resolved on holding their market weekly, and it was accordingly opened on the 27th of June, 1865, and though its success was in some measure impaired by the breaking out of the Cattle Plague, still it may be pronounced now as complete. The first day the new market was opened *out of the town* in 1856, the supply of 2,560 sheep and lambs was considered unusually large, while on Tuesday the 1st of the present month, the weekly supply was 5,110, or nearly double that of the fortnightly supply eleven years ago. Before the market was removed there was not *then* space to get all the stock into the High Street at certain periods of the year; it was held only once a fortnight, and it took two or three days to rid the town of the dirt and annoyance. What would it have been now? That some of the inhabitants were materially injured by the removal there can be no doubt, but had it remained any longer there, it would have greatly curtailed the advancement and general business of the town, and prevented that progress which has been since made. It is now to be hoped that a steady weekly market will more than compensate those who suffered by the removal.

BANKS, ETC.

The Ashford Bank was established by the Messrs. Jemmett in the year 1791, and their place of business was at Messrs. Wilks and Sheppard's surgery, the firm being Jemmett, Whitfeld, and Jemmett. Then it was removed to the late Mr. W. Jemmett's residence, where Mr. Burra, sen. now resides. It was afterwards removed to the house where Mr. Dowsett now carries on his business. The bank

was closed, except on market days, between the hours of one
and two, and only one individual was then required to
transact the whole business of the town. The late Mr.
Simonds was the clerk and manager for several years, and
went to his dinner at one o'clock. One of the most daring
robberies of that period (for even robbers have daily increased in skill) was perpetrated in the year 1823 and the
offenders escaped detection. It is supposed that some
London thieves had by false keys satisfied themselves that
when the bank was closed every evening, the property was
removed for the night to a strong room from the shop now
occupied by Mr. Dowsett to the late Mr. G. E. Jemmett's
house (the present place of business), but that it was not
removed in the middle of the day, and that if they were not
to be foiled, they must enter the premises while Mr.
Simonds was at dinner, and this was at last effected and
everything of any value was taken away. The iron safe in
which the property was kept was again closed by the thieves
and a ring put over the pipe of the lock; thus the time
occupied in forcing open the safe, enabled the thieves to
escape with greater ease. By a compromise with the
thieves the property, except the cash, was afterwards
recovered. On the death of the late Mr. William Jemmett
in December, 1847, a new firm was formed and the valuable
services of the late Mr. Simonds recognised, and he was
admitted as a partner with Mr. Burra, sen. and Mr. G. E.
Jemmett. In the year 1842 the London and County Joint
Stock Bank established a branch here and commenced
business on the premises now occupied by Mr. Jarrett.
The directors subsequently erected their present place of
business. The Ashford Savings Bank was opened on the
3rd of September, 1816. The late Mr. Stephen Tournay
was the first secretary, and held the office until 1825, when
the present secretary, Mr. Thurston, was appointed. The
deposits the first year amounted to £4,000, they now
exceed £46,000 and there are no less than 1,272 depositors.
In the year 1858 a Penny Savings Bank was established and
the deposits amount to £581, and there are 560 depositors.
In the year 1861 a branch of the Post Office Savings Bank
was opened. The Postmaster now collects nearly £1,500

monthly from 920 depositors, and it is estimated that nearly
£30,000 has been deposited at this branch since it was established. In the year 1852 the Ashford Permanent Building
Society was established. There are now three hundred
investing and borrowing members, and the funds of the
society amount to the sum of £25,677. Thus for a period
of more than half a century the banking and monetary
transactions have been carried on in this town through
eventful periods of the wildest speculation, without the
slightest loss to the several investors, and with credit to the
parties concerned, and have proved earthly blessings to all
classes, especially the humbler portion of the community.
This may be considered a bright page in the History of
Ashford. It is also worthy of remark that notwithstanding
the introduction of the Post-office banks no less than
£767,000 is still deposited in the Savings Banks in this
county alone; shewing, notwithstanding all that has trans-
pired, the unabated confidence of the poor in these establishments.

THE LATE MR. CHARLES MERCER.

The late Mr. Charles Mercer, who had been brought up
as a solicitor, and practised in this town, left it to join the
Maidstone Bank in April, 1855, when a public dinner was
given, and a handsome testimonial was presented, to him.
Mr. Mercer was the adviser of Mr. G. E. Jemmett, the Lord
of the Manor, and to his energy and desire to advance
the town, we are indebted, amongst other improvements,
for the formation of Bank Street and that fine wide road
to the station called Elwick Road, which was constructed
in the year 1852. Our energetic townsman, Mr. George
Elliott (whose family have been for so many years connected with this town), in the course of the last year erected
his own dwelling house and four semi-detached villas,
which have added materially to the appearance of this road,
and it is to be hoped they will repay him for his outlay.
Ashford does not require at present any more shops, and
its inhabitants should encourage as much as possible

persons of independent means to take up their residence amongst them.

THE "ASHFORD NEWS."

We must not pass over another event which has added no doubt to the importance of the town: the publication by Mr. Igglesden of the *Ashford News*. The first number of this weekly publication was issued on the 17th of July, 1855, at the small cost of one penny. The fears of many good people that the repeal of the duty on paper and newspapers would, by the introduction of cheap literature, lead to mischief has not been realized. With some few exceptions, the public taste, which, after all, rules such matters, is more opposed to calumny in this, our day, than it was during the first quarter of the present century; and, while the repeal of the duty on beer by the late Duke of Wellington's Government—ostensibly with the object of inducing those in a humble walk of life to brew their own beer and drink it at home—has proved a complete failure, the cheap newspaper and literature of the day have served to cement the domestic tie, and have induced the husband and son to read at home that which they formerly went abroad to read or hear, amidst the excitement of the inn and beer-house. Mr. Igglesden commenced with a small sheet of paper and a circulation of 300 copies, and by steady perseverance and watchfulness, and the able judgment and assistance of his staff, including his chief reporter (Mr. Rutter), he now, with a double sheet of larger dimensions, has increased his weekly circulation to 10,000,ˣand the advertisements have gone on increasing in the same proportion. The following simple fact connected with newspaper reporting will show what great changes take place in the mind of the public even in the course of one generation. A clerk was in the habit of reporting, some thirty years ago, the magisterial proceedings at Ashford to one of the county papers, and of course inserted the names of the Justices present. One highly respectable magistrate, now no more, actually complained of it, and the practice was discontinued. What would the vigilant public now

X 22,850 _____

say if Mr. Rutter was not at his post ? Would they not imagine that something was going on which would not bear the eye of the scrutinizing public ? If not improved in our hearts, we are in our outward daily conduct made more circumspect by this local censorship, and MIGHT is not now so likely to overcome RIGHT.

THE POST OFFICE.

Nor must we forget to notice the great advantages and accommodation which the public have derived in our Post-office arrangements, increased materially by the obliging conduct of Mr. Munns (the present postmaster), who succeeded Mr. Tunbridge in 1859. Forty years ago the postage of a letter to London cost eightpence, and strange to say the postage of a letter to Canterbury, (one-fourth of the distance), cost the same sum. In the year 1839 the penny postage system came into operation—one of the greatest boons to the public in this our day. We should also bear in mind the benefit the public now derive from the improvement in the money order department in the Post-office, and the present book-post system. We have now a letter pillar in New Street ; three daily despatches to London, and three deliveries from London ; two to Dover and Folkestone, and a day mail to Charing, Wye, and Willesborough ; and the latest concession has been an extra evening mail to Rye, Hastings, and Brighton. Some of my audience no doubt remember poor old Harry Lanes, the Eastwell letter carrier, who, though he possessed a weak mind, had a good memory, and his whistling the different tunes played on the chimes in our church was considered perfection.

OTHER PUBLIC INSTITUTIONS.

Deferring for the present our remarks on the Railway and its Works here, I will in the meantime comment briefly on matters of minor importance. Our Fairs of ancient origin fortunately have of late been held out of the town, and as the occasion for them has long since ceased, they ought to be suppressed. The oldest literary society which we have is the Book Club, established in the year 1815, which combines good fellowship with the improvement of the mind. It has held its own for more than fifty years, which of itself is a sufficient commendation in this changeable world, and in 1865 its members commemorated their jubilee by a fete in Eastwell Park. Mr. John Bayley is its senior member. There were horse races here in 1829, which were held at Ripton, and were supported by the late Earls of Thanet, but which have long since been discontinued. Our Whitsuntide holiday has supplied the place of the races. An agricultural society was established in the year 1834, at the time of the change in the Poor Laws. The society was intended for the encouragement of agricultural labourers, and was given up in 1861, when it was considered that its object had been accomplished, and the Christmas Cattle Show was introduced as a substitute. To this was added last year a Poultry Show, which bids fair to be a success. We must also mention the two good Mechanics' Institutes with libraries, containing together nearly 3,000 volumes of books. We have also two good reading rooms, where nearly all the daily papers may be seen—one at the Public Rooms, and the other at the New Town. Mr. Henry Whitfeld, (the President of the Ashford Institute), is ever ready to cater for a winter evening's amusement. We have also an old established Fire Engine Association, which, it is too much, perhaps, the fashion to abuse, considering the services of the members are voluntary. Water Works were established here in 1853, and have been thus far less successful than most of our other undertakings. They are deserving the best consideration of the well-wishers of our town. We must not forget the improvements at the corner of Castle Street, through the exertions of Mr. Burra, sen. We may also be proud of the 29th Kent Volunteers, established here, for defence and not defiance, on the 29th December, 1859. The Justices Court House and Police Station were erected in 1864. The Petty Sessions, thirty years ago, were always held at the Saracen's Head. The old Saracen's Head (the original site of the dwelling house of the Lord of the Manor) was taken down in 1862 and the commodious

hotel erected, and North Street widened in that year. Our
Choral Society was established in 1865, with every desire to
foster the little musical talent at present existing in the
town. The ornamental building for the Billiard Club was
erected in the present year ; and I suppose almost the last,
but not to my mind the least, important recent event which
I have to record, is the opening of the public Swimming
Bath, which is calculated, as I believe, to be of essential
service to the rising generation.

I omitted, in reading this address, to state that the Act
for the more easy recovery of small debts, was passed in
August, 1846, and came into operation in 1847. A district
was assigned to Ashford, and Mr. A. Dangerfield is the
registrar of this district.

THE RAILWAY.

We have passed hastily over all these improvements and
changes, and we will now turn our thoughts to the great
pivot upon which the prosperity and extension of our town
turned, viz., the construction of the South Eastern Railway.
Shortly after Mr. Stevenson had opened the Manchester
and Liverpool Railway, he commenced the little railway
from Whitstable to Canterbury, parts of which were
originally worked by fixed engines, and the remainder by
locomotive power. A bill had been obtained for the construction of a railway from London to Croydon, and the
South Eastern company then introduced a bill for a railway
from Croydon to Dover. The promoters would have made
this line through the principal towns of Kent, but they
were so strongly opposed by the landowners, innkeepers,
post horse and stage coach proprietors, that they abandoned
their plan, and availing themselves of the assistance of one
of the then members for the county (the late Mr. Hodges),
who saw the great advantages which would arise to the
Weald of Kent, they ultimately succeeded in ob-
taining their act, which received the royal assent
on the 21st June, 1836, and it is to the passing of
this act that Ashford owes its present position. Another
company had obtained an act for the construction of a

railway to Brighton. This company by a subsequent arrangement completed the line to Red Hill, and the South Eastern company carried it on from Red Hill to Dover. This line was opened as far as Tunbridge on the 26th of May, 1842, and to Headcorn on the 31st August, 1842, and stage coaches were allowed to pass from Ashford through Sir Edward Dering's grounds to Headcorn, until the 1st of December, 1842, when the line was opened to Ashford. This is nearly twenty-five years ago. The public from Canterbury and the coast then travelled by the different turnpike roads to Ashford. This for a short time caused a great deal of bustle here. On the 28th of June, 1843, the line was opened to Folkestone, and on the 7th February, 1844, the main line to Dover was completed and opened. The branch to Canterbury was opened in July, 1846; to Ramsgate, July, 1847; and to Rye, February, 1851. To perfect our railway communication we only now require a branch to Maidstone, for which an act has been obtained, but there is no prospect of the work being commenced until the money market becomes more settled, and a fresh spirit of enterprise arises. These lines and branches however, would not have so materially increased the population and importance of the town had it not been for the establishment of the permanent works of the company here. The Directors were undecided as to where these works should be constructed, when the late Mr. Wall consented to sell a large portion of his land for this purpose, and that settled the question. The buildings were proceeded with at once, and in the month of July, 1847 (twenty years ago), the mechanics commenced working in the shops. There are now more than 1,200 men employed in these works, 1,100 in the locomotive and carriage departments in about equal proportions, and more than 130 in the engineers', station, and telegraph departments, under the able superintendence of Mr. Cudworth and Mr. Mansell, who, notwithstanding the many changes in the directory, have retained their appointments and discharged their respective duties to the satisfaction of their employers and the public. But in closing these remarks on the railway, I must not pass by our highly respected station master, Mr. Wedderburn, who

came amongst us more than five-and-twenty years ago,
while the works were in the course of construction, and
remains to this day a living proof that by strict integrity,
punctuality, and sobriety, a man may serve faithfully his
employers and retain their confidence, and at the same time
enjoy the good opinion of the public, who have *once* recognised the value of his services, and if I am not mistaken,
much time will not elapse before they will be ready to do it
a *second* time; for not a single collision or accident during
his long services, can, I believe, be attributed to him.
Pause for one moment,—twenty-five years ago, two coaches
containing at the utmost sixteen passengers each, and a van
containing eight passengers, formed the only daily pas-
senger traffic to and from London (except posting), and
now watch the arrival and departure of each train at our
station, and behold the busy multitude thronging our plat-
forms. Are we not living in a migratory age?

SANATORIUM AND DISPENSARY.

The cry of the world is " Onward," and if I may be per-
mitted to say what I think we most want at the present
time, it is a good Dispensary. Mr. Henry Whitfeld kindly
opened in 1860, at his sole cost, a Sanatorium, and has expended on it upwards of £400; but as a lawyer does not
often take for granted the law of his professional opponent,
so I fear a doctor does not often like physic from another
doctor's surgery: hence it is that this building is not ap-
preciated so much as it ought to be. The staff of medical
men in this town are a talented body, and if they would
only unite to establish a Dispensary, I feel confident that,
with the assistance of the neighbouring gentry and clergy,
we ought, with our increasing population, to establish a good
one; and I know of no better site for it than the piece of
spare land in North Street, at the corner of Park Street.

THE TOWN AND ITS INMATES.

I think that Ashford should be a happy town. If you
ask me why? my answer is: Because almost all its popu-

lation follow some daily calling, and ever remember there is as much religion in week-day labour, properly sanctified, as in the due observance of the Sabbath. The idle hand is too often the mischievous one. There has been a general desire here to keep pace with the times and improve our buildings and shops. Who would have supposed that the little business carried on in New Rents by the late Mr. Rogers, would in thirty years have grown to such magnitude as it has under the energetic Mr. G. A. Lewis ?

We have here co-operative societies ; but, thank God, we have no Sheffield saw-grinders or Stockport brickmakers, but a body of 1,200 skilful men, old and young, engaged in daily labour, whose conduct in public and private life is as creditable to them, as it is to their employers, and I really believe there is less drunkenness and cursing and swearing in Ashford at this time, than there was before these mechanics settled amongst us. It is worthy of remark that not a single official charge has been made against any publican or retailer of beer in this town during the last year. All praise to those inhabitants who have laboured so hard in the cause of temperance.

Again, Ashford is as healthy a town as any in Kent, standing on rising ground, with a spacious High Street, possessing every advantage for proper drainage, with a pretty little stream (alas, too much polluted), surrounded by green pastures, and belted by Eastwell Park and the Wye Downs, with all their varied beauties.

CLERGY, PLACES OF WORSHIP, CEMETERY, ETC.

Let us now for a few moments direct our thoughts to our clergy, our places of worship, and our schools. The living of Ashford is a vicarage in the gift of the Dean and Chapter of Rochester. The rectorial tithes were held for many years under lease from the Dean and Chapter, by the family of the late Earl of Thanet, and are now held by Admiral Marsham and Captain Styles. The late respected vicar of Ashford (the Rev. Thomas Wood), died on the 23rd November, 1847, (almost twenty years ago), and was succeeded by the present vicar, the Rev. J. P. Alcock, since appointed a Rural Dean and one of the hon. Canons of Canterbury, who has devoted his time and energies for the good of his parishioners during the whole of this period. It is to our present vicar we owe the establishment of our District Visiting Society; until this was done, the greatest beggars got the greatest assistance, but now every case is investigated by the ladies who so kindly assist in the good work, and every subscriber may refer each applicant for aid to the visitor of the district in which the party resides, with the satisfaction of feeling that the case will not be neglected. This society provides food for the soul as well as the body. A branch society has been established in South Ashford, and ours is the pleasing task this evening to endeavour to assist its funds. It is to our vicar also, with the co-operation of his then churchwarden, the late Mr. Charles Mercer, that we are indebted for the great improvements in the chancel of our church, and to him and subsequent churchwardens for the judicious alterations and enlargement of the body of the church. If any proof of his perseverance is required we have only to point to the New Church at South Ashford, which was opened on the 1st May, in the present year, the Rev. P. J. Syrèe having undertaken the charge of the district. Mr. Alcock, single handed, circulated about 12,000 letters, and succeeded in collecting about £4,000 from 1,000 individuals, scattered over England.

Almost every denomination of Christians has a place of worship here, and some of them more than one. The late Mr. Betts erected the present Wesleyan Chapel at his own cost, on the completion of the railway to Ashford. The Roman Catholics erected a chapel at Barrow Hill, which was opened on the 22nd of August, 1865. The Independents have lately erected a Congregational Church, which was opened on the 1st of February, 1866. The Wesleyans and Baptists each contemplate building a new chapel here.

In the year 1857, the different places of burial were closed by an order from the Secretary of State, and the New Cemetery on the Canterbury road, was formally opened on the 5th of May, 1860. We may be partial, but **we think there is not** a prettier one in the county. Much of that gloom surrounding our places of sepulture, which our ancestors delighted in, is daily disappearing, and the hope beyond the grave is, we trust, growing stronger.

EDUCATION.

Of our schools, it is rather singular that thus far our upper and middle class schools have gone back, while our town has gone forward ; and now, while the mastership of our Grammar School is vacant by the lamented death of the Rev. Mr. Wright, the spirited inhabitants and fathers of families may, with advantage, endeavour to get a re arrangement of the property, and, either by subscription or shares, erect a suitable residence and repair the school, and thereby secure the services of a well qualified master; for Ashford, from its position and the advantages of the railway, ought to be able to support a good Grammar School. Our National School was first opened in 1816, behind the workhouse and on the site of the Fire Engine House. It was ill adapted for the requirements of the town, and a large bazaar was held at Godinton on the 23rd September, 1840, to raise funds for a new building. The late Earl and Countess of Winchilsea and other county families took part in this proceeding, a considerable sum was collected, and the foundation stone of the school was laid on the 8th June, 1841, by the present Mrs. Toke. The South Eastern company subsequently erected a school on their locomotive establishment ; both schools are admirably conducted. The rising generation of the poor are deeply indebted to our Vicar for all he has done towards securing them a good education, and his endeavours afterwards to push the young people into the world are deserving of praise. In these two establishments there are at present 902 children deriving a sound, scriptural, and useful education, commencing and ending their daily work with prayer. We have here also well managed British Schools. There are 503 children on their books. The present schools were opened on the 14th of February, 1862, at a cost of £1405. Popular as these schools are becoming, I cannot as yet bring my mind to support them. The Ashford British

Schools are no doubt good of their kind; but, I still feel the religious instruction is too limited, and in endeavouring to convey this instruction to the children, there is too great a fear, as it appears to me, of giving it a sectarian character. Thus, when the Bible is read there is the chance of its being too often treated as any ordinary book would be. Why the infant school *only* is opened and closed with prayer, I cannot understand. When the Government Inspector comes down not one question I believe is put by him to the children on any religious subject, and thus the most important end, as I think, of all education is lost sight of. I have supported for many years the British and Foreign Bible Society, which disperses the Sacred Word in all languages, without note or comment, and without regard to sect or party, still I have ever felt that to give force and power to this sacred book, there must be teachers, missionaries, and interpreters of it; and in what place can this be so properly done as in a school-room? When Philip asked the Ethiopian whether he understood what he was reading? he answered, "How can I, except some man should guide me." We know, alas, that this instruction is not given at home, but we are told that the different ministers and their teachers do this on the Sabbath; but if the children will not regularly attend Sunday Schools (too often the case), when do they get this religious instruction? Sunday teaching is only a make-shift, and was only really popular when we had no daily instruction. It is gradually losing its hold on the dissenter as well as the churchman. Giving all the credit to the managers of the British School in this town which they are entitled to, I must respectfully express my dissent to any system of education which is so secular. What was the command of the Almighty to the children of Israel? " Ye shall lay up these my words in your heart and in your soul, and bind them for a sign upon your hand, that they may be as frontlets between your eyes. And ye shall teach them your children, speaking of them when thou sittest in thine house, and when thou walkest by the way; when thou liest down and when thou risest up. And thou shalt write them upon the door-posts of thine house, and upon thy gates." Don't wait until the mind has ceased to be plastic, but after being taught yourselves, you are to teach these words to your children. Walk down the High Street of Ashford after sunset on any Friday evening, and you will find the shop No. 23, closed, and kept so until the sunset of Saturday evening. From this trifling circumstance the Ashford sceptic may witness with his own eyes some of the best evidence of the truth and authenticity of the Bible. Contrast this Jewish faith with the following specimen of modern infidelity, "Not many weeks ago the students at Liege, in Belgium, passed a resolution in favor of atheism." What religious instruction could these unhappy young men have had? Remember, I am not making these remarks with any hostile or proselyting spirit. I am never induced to prize a school for the number of its attendants. I would rather see a less number well instructed, than a crowded school not half attended to. Remember also that what is well instilled in youth, is always the longest retained. Are we to educate for time only? In short, is eternity to have the first, second, or no place in modern instruction? *This is the great question of the day*, and if the churchman and dissenter can only be induced to stand side by side, there is no fear as to what the answer will be! But I am dwelling too long on a subject ever near to my heart.

POLITICAL AND RELIGIOUS POSITION.

I must now turn to our political and religious position. There is no country in the world where there is a greater amount of liberty enjoyed by its people than in England, and there are but few places of the same size where the inhabitants use that liberty in political, as well as in religious matters, with less control than Ashford. It may hitherto have been a thriving town, if it is not a wealthy one. The influence of money or territorial possessions is not brought to bear on the political opinions of its inhabitants. But whether in things affecting time or eternity where would England have been without a vigilant public? We are all the better for being looked after. What would the Church of England have been without dissent? And where would dissent have been with the Church of Rome in the place of the Church of England? I am firmly attached to my own church, but this should not make me intolerant. We have now, it is supposed, a population of more than 8,000. Can a vicar and two curates and two buildings, capable of holding only a fourth of this population, be deemed sufficient for the spiritual necessities of this town? If churchmen are torpid, why cavil at the erection of new chapels, and the exertions of nonconformist ministers? Is there not enough for all to do? Does the intolerant churchman, who expects a good seat in his parish church, and does not contribute one sixpence towards the support of the ministry, or the education of the poor, suppose that he is properly upholding that church? Or can the clamorous dissenter believe that the chapel which he frequents, will thrive a jot more should he ever succeed in his daily exertions to overthrow that church? Should it be a subject of controversy whether a body should moulder into dust in the consecrated or unconsecrated portion of our cemetery; while perhaps the soul which has quitted that earthly tabernacle, might have been better watched over and cared for when on earth? I have no doubt that our clergy and the different ministers of religion are often sadly imposed upon, and the desire to obtain bodily sustenance frequently causes the poor to represent themselves as either members of the church, or nonconformists, as it suits their purpose, and thus as they call it, divide their favors. A worse system cannot be encouraged, especially as it produces a collision between the clergy and dissenting ministers. It would, however, be soon checked and kept under control, and the impostors detected if there was a better understanding between these gentlemen. Is the line of separation still to continue as it did in our Saviour's time, when the Jews had no dealings with the Samaritans? If so, don't forget that in two of our Lord's most beautiful parables, the Samaritan is held up for our example. Can those we so often hear raving against dissent, shut their eyes to the fact that many a nonconformist by the simple single-mindedness of his piety, puts the professing churchman to the blush? Do we not all constantly forget that God's church is one family? It has been well-said that the more men think, the more they will differ, and in nothing is this so apparent as in matters of religion, and this difference will continue until the churchman and dissenter both devote themselves heartily to Christ, and then, and not till then, will the walls of separation be broken down.

I had written the foregoing remarks before I read the tolerant speech of the Bishop of Oxford to the working men of Wolverhampton. Surely the reverend prelate must have startled some of his admirers! His conversion must have been almost as sudden as that of the present Government on the question of Reform, for he told the meeting that "if the Church was to fulfil her mission she must display a greater liberality towards dissenters," and he condemned the wretched jealousies of conflicting sects. Is not this the feeling of every tolerant churchman?

OUR HOMES.

I have already endeavoured to point out that your Local Board is comparatively powerless in sanitary matters, without the co-operation of the inhabitants in keeping their homes free from impurities. Now, permit me as a friend and neighbour to say that we cannot keep our souls free from the defilements of sin and the pollution of the world, without the aid of the Holy Spirit which is promised to us if we seek it. An Englishman's home is his castle; but that castle should be defended from within as well as from without, if it is to resist an enemy. If in this life peace, contentment, and happiness are ever to be found, they will be found in our homes, but they will not tarry there long if our Bibles lie on our tables for ornament and not for use.

Externally the Sabbath is well observed here, and there is no open violation of it in our streets; but is it properly observed in our homes? We are *all* fellow laborers. Do we hail the first day of the week as a day of holy rest? If we do, we shall make it so to our dependents, and see that our children keep it properly. Those who have experienced it, can never sufficiently appreciate the advantage derived from a parent's Sabbath instruction. The youth may wander; but, oh, if the seed is only properly sown, who shall measure the mercy and goodness of God through Christ, and at one time or another in after life the wanderer will return to the fold of the Good Shepherd.

It is a cause for thankfulness that the Almighty has put it into the hearts of many laymen in the present day who have been working hard throughout the week, to labour on the Sabbath for the extension of Christ's kingdom; and here let me mention with grateful thanks the name of Mr. W. H. Baker, who has for many years been daily employed at the South Eastern Works in a very simple department. He deserves better employment, but he has learnt that Godliness with contentment is great gain. This worthy man devotes his Sunday evenings in visiting the lodging houses in this town and reading and expounding the Scriptures, and praying with the unhappy and degraded inmates; and he oftentimes secures the attention of between twenty and thirty of them. May the Lord reward him for it. Let us one and all remember that if our daily engagements prevent our assisting in instructing the poor and ignorant, and visiting and providing for the sick and needy, we should each, according to our means, cheerfully contribute towards paying for the services of those who are employed to do it. Who is it you will ask who thus ventures to admonish you? My answer is, a fellow sinner.

CONCLUSION.

But I must close these reflections. I have briefly and in chronological order (as far as it was practicable) endeavoured to bring under your notice the leading events which have occurred in this town during the present century. I trust they will not be altogether useless and uninteresting to the majority of those present. The dates I have furnished will, it is hoped be of service, especially to the rising generation. Many and great are our unmerited blessings, and I wish to impress on my own mind as well as yours, never to be weary of well doing, and never to rely entirely on our own might and strength. Ever remembering that "Both riches and honor come of Thee O Lord, and Thou reignest over all."

NOTE.—Under the head of Banks, &c., I find I omitted to state that there was another private bank which was carried on by the late Mr. Edward Stoddart, up to the year 1829, at Dr. Beet's present surgery, and the late Mr. John Hutton was a partner in the firm.

THE END.

POSTCRIPT.

THE ASHFORD BRITISH SCHOOLS.

As I was to some extent ignorant of the system of religious education adopted at the British Schools, I requested the secretary (the Rev. Mr. Turner), while preparing my address, to supply me with answers to the following questions :—

1.—The religious course of instruction at the British Schools ?

2.—What portion of the day is devoted to the study of the scriptures ?

3.—Whether the scriptures are expounded ?

4.—Whether the Government Inspector examines the children on religious subjects ?

He kindly furnished me with the following replies, written, I believe, by the master of the British Schools :—

BOYS.—The school is opened each day with the reading of a portion of scripture by the teacher. In the upper part of the school, including sections 1 and 2, (about half the scholars), each boy has daily to commit to memory a text of scripture. In section 1, there are weekly, two bible-reading lessons of nearly an hour; which are supplemented by oral instruction, as to the geography of the places mentioned, or any remarkable historical incidents which may be calculated to elucidate the narrative. But no comments are made calculated to give a sectarian character to the instruction. In section 2, three times weekly, the New Testament is read for nearly an hour. These lessons are afterwards questioned upon by the teacher. In sections 3 and 4, many of their reading lessons are of a religious character; such for instance as those in the books published by the Irish Board.

GIRLS.—In the girls' school, the instruction of a religious character is similar.

INFANTS.—The school is opened and closed with prayer; and the children have an oral lesson daily on some portion of scripture; care being taken to select those parts which can be comprehended by, and will interest children of such an age. Pains are taken on all fitting occasions to impress upon the minds of the children the *moral* teachings of the bible in each school.

The Government Inspector does not examine the school in religious subjects; the managers have to certify that they are satisfied with the religious instruction.

Now, if I have in the foregoing remarks unintentionally drawn erroneous conclusions from these replies, I deeply regret it. The public must judge between us. As, however, I hope through life to advocate fair play and justice, I have consented to attach to this address the following defence of their system, prepared by the Ashford Committee of the British Schools.

"The British School Committee feel that Mr. Furley, in the paper read before the Mechanics' Institute, has unintentionally misrepresented the religious aspect of those schools by saying ' that the religious teaching is too limited, that there is too great a fear of giving it a sectarian character! Thus when the Bible is read there is the chance of its being too often treated as an ordinary book.' He also complains because the Government Inspector does not examine the schools on religious subjects, and that more prayer is not used; drawing the conclusion that the spiritual well-being of the scholars is thereby neglected, conveying the idea by the whole tenor of his remarks that British schools are ' so secular' and confined to the affairs of this life that the commands of the Almighty (which he quotes) are set aside, to the great peril of the childrens' highest interest. The committee deeply regret that Mr. Furley should, without better knowledge of facts, and without personal inspection, have ventured on such assertions. The religious instruction in these schools is not founded on any catechism or humanly-compiled formula, like those used in

National schools; the Bible is read and expounded in a way suited to the capacities of children, and with a view to informing their minds on its general teaching, including its geographical, historical, and spiritual bearing; and hence the religious teaching is far less limited than it could be if given from a catechism, or any human compilation; and we believe, if facts could be collated, that this mode of imparting religious truth is more influential for good than the mode adopted in National schools; and the care taken not to give a sectarian bias to the education we consider a merit, from the fact that the schools are *British*, the constitution of England being to leave all at liberty to form their denominational views; and the danger of treating the Bible as a common book is removed from the fact of its being used in the school for a specific purpose, not as a task, but as informing the mind on divine things. It will, therefore, be readily seen why the Government Inspector does not examine the school in religious subjects. In National schools he has the Catechism to guide him, and his questions are necessarily based upon its contents, and hence, whatsoever the religious opinions of the Inspector, he can only put such questions to the school as the Catechism contains, or such as can be readily answered from its teaching; but no such formula being used in British schools, it will at once be seen that no inspection can take place without exposing the school to the peculiar bias of the examiner, who may be a Unitarian, or Roman Catholic, or of religious opinions quite opposite to those of the committee, who consider that the religious teaching can be better controlled by them than by the Government Inspector. Mr. Furley feels, and hence writes, as a Churchman, and we are convinced has no wish or intention to injure any useful institution, but his limited knowledge of the state of schools other than National has led him into serious error, which is evident by his sentiments on Sunday schools, representing them as 'only makeshifts,' and as losing their hold on Dissenters as well as Churchmen. We have pleasure in informing Mr. Furley that enquiries have been made at the Ashford British schools, and it is found that of 208 boys and girls present, 167, or, four-fifths, belonged to some Sunday school. Prayer is not excluded from the day schools. The teachers may, if they feel disposed, at any time open or close, or conduct a devotional exercise; many prefer, however, to read the devotional parts of scripture instead, having no written form of prayer supplied them. The committee and teachers, Mr. Furley will thus learn, have been acting in harmony with his advice, and 'not waited until the mind has ceased to be plastic,' but having been taught themselves, have taught divine truth to the children; and they hope ever to render the schools, both in their secular and religious teaching, worthy of that large measure of public support they are now receiving."